You can learn more about Author Tania Giguere at Tania's Field of Dreams, Facebook, Amazon Author Pages, Pinterest, Twitter, Tumblr, and Goodreads.

Publishing History

Caves Of Wonder Paperback

First Addition 2018

ISBN-13: 978-1722329334

***

CAVES OF WONDER

***

Tania Giguere

A cave is natural chamber or a series of chambers that form underground. It is a space, large enough for a man to enter. Caves are usually, formed naturally, by the weathering of rock and often extend deep underground. Cave refers to a small opening at the top which widens the farther down you travel, making for an exciting adventure. And a cavern is a particular type of cave, and it is naturally, formed in the soluble rock. And when you are exploring caves for recreation, it is called caving.

Speleology is the science of exploration and is the study of all perspectives of the environment.

Marble Cave Undermines

Marble Cave

Antelope Canyon

Nature Rock Cave

Sea Caves Nature Erosion

Ice Cave

Cave Waterfall Inside

Cave Grotto

Stalactite Cave

Rock Cave Nature

Cave Rock Guilin Stone

Cave Sand Stone Nature

Cave Tunnel Underground Entrance

Sea Lions Cave

Cavern Underground Nature

Underground Cave Stalactites

Cave

Mountains Snow Cave

Leaf Nosed Bats Cave

Tree Cave Forest

Crab Cave Underwater

Bat Cave

Nature

Sea Cave

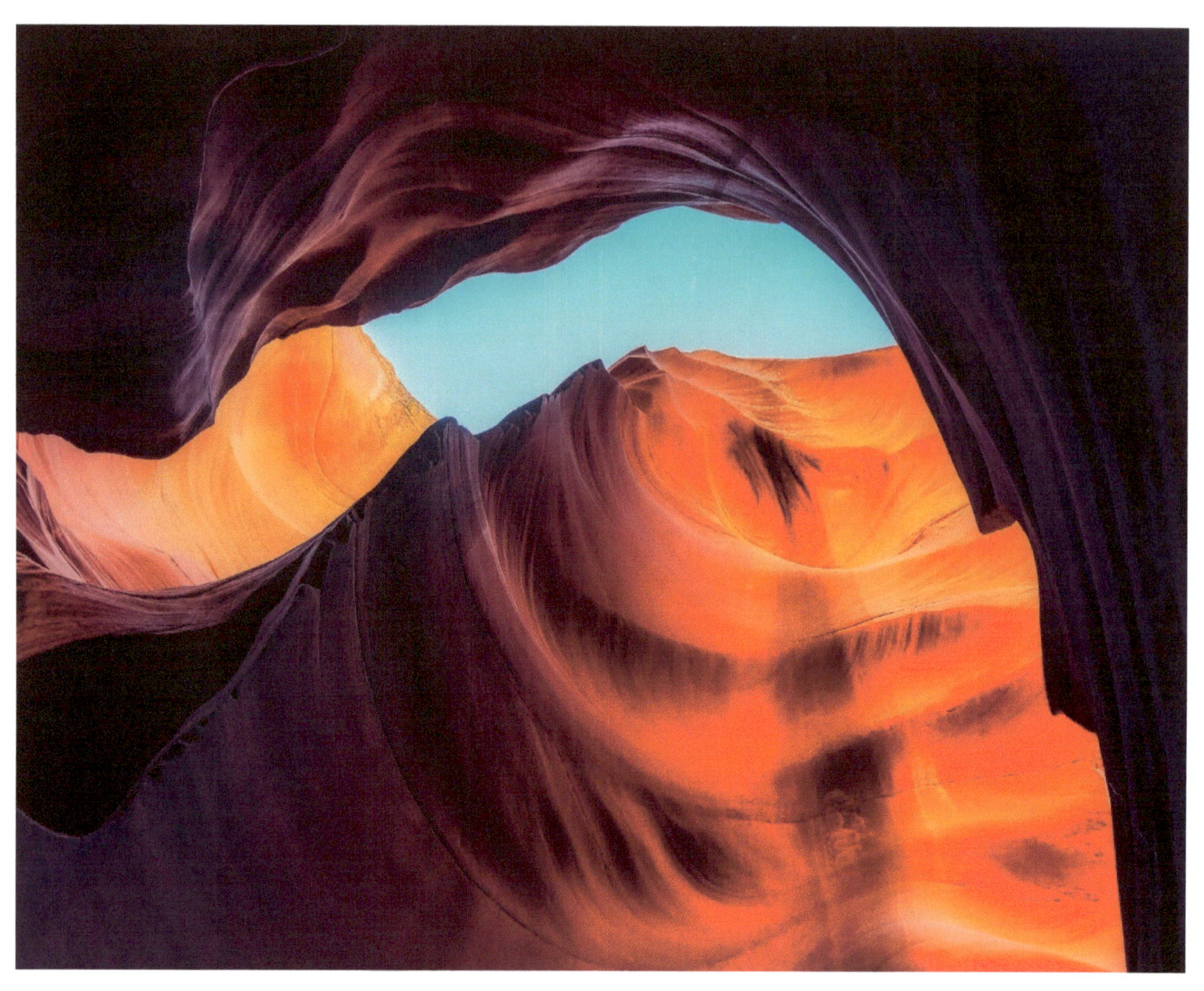

Arizona Arches Canyon Desert

Canyon Red Sand Stone

Glen Canyon Utah

Cave Small Waterfall Nature

Italy Cave

Speleothems Cave Underground Nature

Cave Rock Stone Landform

Cave Rock Stone Underground

Tawny Owl Tree Cave

Penguin Water Bird Cave Nesting Place

Sea Lions Cave Oregon

Sea Cave

Spring Water Cave

Stream Water Cave

Valley Of Roses Cappadocia Passage Cave

Cave Entrance

Whitetip Reef Shark Cave Small

Marmot Stones Cave

Valkenburg Caves Underground

Icicle Bird Stove Cave

Cave Stalactite

Canyon Red Rocks

Sea Cave Entrance

Nature

Seashore

Landscape Sea

Hiking Trail

River Canyon Evening

Country Road

Railroad Tunnel

Young Bear Living In A Cave

Caves Rock Mountain Red Sandstone

Ant Cave

Underground Cave

Ice Cave Glacier

Ruin Cave

Desert Hiking

Travel The Water

Reflect

Enjoy The Wonder

Climb To New Heights

Peaceful And Silent

Live For Today

Ruby Falls Under Lookout Mountain

Chillagoe Caves

Underground Cave Lighted

 Long ago caves were used by people for plenty of reasons they provided shelter, and for some people, they were a source of minerals and economic prosperity.

So now you have seen the unseen, and it is a wondrous place filled with magic. It fills your heart with envy and clouds your mind with undecided thoughts. Should I be that explorer or should I stay and be the watcher?

Only you can make the changes in your life.